BAS ITNI SI BAAT

MUNTAZIR

notionpress
.com

INDIA • SINGAPORE • MALAYSIA

ISBN
Paperback 979-8-90431-510-8
Hardcase 979-8-90431-511-5

Dedicated to my,

Anam Cara…

May you find the peace,

that always alluded me.

CONTENTS

ACKNOWLEDGEMENTS...

I owe this book to my wife, Pooja. She held the fort so I could fight the battles.

To my son, Manthan. It is an honor and a privilege to watch him grow.

To my sister, Priyanka, the one person I could burn the world for.

To my parents, for doing their best to raise me and for giving me all that I have.

FIRAAQ फ़िराक़

Dhundte rehte hain kuch,
Kabhi aatish, toh kabhi rakh mein,

Rote hain aksar hum,
Kabhi fikr, toh kabhi firaaq mein.

ढूँढते रहते हैं कुछ – कभी आतिश, तो कभी राख में,

रोते हैं अक्सर हम – कभी फ़िक्र, तो कभी फ़िराक़ में।

Karam...

Yun hi kharochta gaya, dil main koi zakhm na tha,
Mehfil se nikal gaya, mere taur ka koi bazm na tha,

Farishton sa wo sab ke dard seh leta hai,
Ek mere liye unn ke dil main koi Reham na tha,

Tumhara dil rakkhne tumhein dua main maanga nahi,
Warna khuda na nawazein mujhpe aise koi karam na tha,

Tumhara bin batayein chala jaana kha gaya mujhe,
Yu mera dil tod sakein aisa koi sitam na tha,

Main chonk gaya jab meri aawaz unchi ho gayi,
Apki batsalukhi se mujhe koi vehem na tha,

Muntazir log mujhe apna aashiq kehte rehte hai,
Main sach Kahn toh main kabhi kisi ka sanam na tha,

करम...

यूँ ही खरोंचता गया, दिल में कोई ज़ख्म न था,
महफ़िल से निकल गया, मेरे तौर का कोई बज़्म न था,
फ़रिश्तों सा वो सबके दर्द सह लेता है,
एक मेरे लिए उन के दिल में कोई रहम न था,
तुम्हारा दिल रखने तुम्हें दुआ में माँगा नहीं,
वरना ख़ुदा न नवाज़ें मुझपे ऐसा कोई करम न था,
तुम्हारा बिन बताए चला जाना खा गया मुझे,
यूँ मेरा दिल तोड़ सकें ऐसा कोई सितम न था,
मैं चौंक गया जब मेरी आवाज़ ऊँची हो गई,
आपकी बदसलूकी से मुझे कोई वहम न था,
मुन्तज़िर लोग मुझे अपना आशिक़ कहते रहते हैं,
मैं सच कहूँ तो मैं कभी किसी का सनम न था।

Dost...

Ek awaaz pe aayein — saare dost milne aayein,
Apno ke dhokhe kha kar mujh gair ko sambhalne aayein.

Saare yaar tohfon mein teri baatein hi laayein,
Janamdin par bhi aakar mujhe rulaane aayein.

Main intezaar mein baitha hoon tera rumaal liye,
Be-mann hi sahi — tu meri aankhein sukhane aayein.

Aane wale duniya-e-baghaawat kar ke aayein,
Tere khat mein na aane ke bas bahaane laayein.

Ye ibaadat ki jagah hai — tum faqat gham kyun laayein?
Jab peete nahin ho, bolo kyun maikhane aayein?

Humein ilm hota toh hum yahan kabhi na aatein,
Na jaane kis ka karz utarne is jahan mein aayein.

दोस्त...

एक आवाज़ पे आएँ – सारे दोस्त मिलने आएँ,
अपनों के धोखे खा कर मुझ ग़ैर को संभालने आएँ।

सारे यार तोहफ़ों में तेरी बातें ही लाएँ,
जन्मदिन पर भी आकर मुझे रुलाने आएँ।

मैं इंतज़ार में बैठा हूँ तेरा रुमाल लिए,
बे-मन ही सही – तू मेरी आँखें सुखाने आएँ।

आने वाले दुनिया-ए-बग़ावत कर के आएँ,
तेरे ख़त में ना आने के बस बहाने लाएँ।

ये इबादत की जगह है – तुम फ़क़त ग़म क्यों लाएँ?
जब पीते नहीं हो, बोलो क्यों मैख़ाने आएँ?

हमें इल्म होता तो हम यहाँ कभी ना आते,
ना जाने किस का कर्ज़ उतारने इस जहाँ में आएँ।

Bhool Jaana...

Unka ek hunar hai — har baat bhool jaana,
Kehte kehte baat koi, woh baat bhool jaana.

June ka mahina tha, baadal ghane-ghane the,
Hum saath naache the — woh barsaat bhool jaana.

December ki thand aur woh haathon ko sekna,
Humne kaati thi jo raat — woh raat bhool jaana.

Kahin ka nahin rehta jo ishq se ishq kar le,
Bada aasaan hai ishq mein insaan ki zaat bhool jaana.

Jagah, taarikh, shakl, vaadein, tohfe bhool gaya main,
Mushkil hai magar woh aakhri mulaqaat bhool jaana.

Tum kaho toh main apna naam tak bhool jaaun,
Par mujhse na hoga woh pal, woh jazbaat bhool jaana.

भूल जाना...

उनका एक हुनर है – हर बात भूल जाना,
कहते कहते बात कोई, वो बात भूल जाना।

जून का महीना था, बादल घने-घने थे,
हम साथ नाचे थे – वो बरसात भूल जाना।

दिसंबर की ठंड और वो हाथों को सेकना,
हमने काटी थी जो रात – वो रात भूल जाना।

कहीं का नहीं रहता जो इश्क़ से इश्क़ कर ले,
बड़ा आसान है इश्क़ में इंसान की ज़ात भूल जाना।

जगह, तारीख़, शक्ल, वादे, तोहफ़े भूल गया मैं,
मुश्किल है मगर वो आख़िरी मुलाक़ात भूल जाना।

तुम कहो तो मैं अपना नाम तक भूल जाऊँ,
पर मुझसे न होगा वो पल, वो जज़्बात भूल जाना।

Pareshani...

Yun toh sab theek hai — par na jaane kya pareshani hai,
Shayad mujhe bimaari hai, ya shauqiya pareshani hai.

Main poochta reh gaya, woh rota raha raat bhar,
Subah jaate jaate keh gaya — ishq jaavedaani hai.

Roothne-manaane ke khel ka kya nateeja nikla, yaad nahin,
Log kehte rahe — ye pyaar nahin, umr ki nadaani hai.

Main hoon kahan — na jaane kaafir, momin ya saaqi,
Masjid, galli ya mehkhaana — kaho, kahan meri jawaani hai?

Jo zinda hai woh jaane, jis pe beeti wohi jaanta hai,
Jo sunta kissa mera, kahe — ye manghadat kahaani hai.

Main jee raha hoon ab tak — zindagi bhi hairaan hai,
Main marr raha hoon roz kitna — maut ko bhi hairaani hai.

Muntazir, kuch toh socho — ab toh thodi gairat khaao,
Unke qadam jahan padein, wahin rakh di peshani hai.

परेशानी...

यूँ तो सब ठीक है – पर न जाने क्या परेशानी है,
शायद मुझे बीमारी है, या शौक़िया परेशानी है।

मैं पूछता रह गया, वो रोता रहा रात भर,
सुबह जाते-जाते कह गया – इश्क़ जावेदानी है।

रूठने-मनाने के खेल का क्या नतीजा निकला, याद नहीं,
लोग कहते रहे – ये प्यार नहीं, उम्र की नादानी है।

मैं हूँ कहाँ – न जाने काफ़िर, मोमिन या साक़ी,
मस्जिद, गली या मैख़ाना – कहो, कहाँ मेरी जवानी है?

जो ज़िंदा है वो जाने, जिस पे बीती वही जानता है,
जो सुनता किस्सा मेरा, कहे – ये मनगढ़ंत कहानी है।

मैं जी रहा हूँ अब तक – ज़िंदगी भी हैरान है,
मैं मर रहा हूँ रोज़ कितना – मौत को भी हैरानी है।

मुन्तज़िर, कुछ तो सोचो – अब तो थोड़ी ग़ैरत खाओ,
उनके क़दम जहाँ पड़ें, वहीं रख दी पेशानी है।

Theek Ho?...

"Ji, theek ho?"
"Haan, theek hoon."

"Ji, kha liya khana?"
"Haan ji, bas abhi."

"Ji, sambhal ke jaana."
"Ji, zaroor."

Pata nahin kab hamaari baatein
Yun sirf sawaal-jawaab ban gayin.

Abhi toh mile hi the na —
Dost the… aur phir ajnabi ban gaye.

Woh haal poochhte hain,
Main kehta hoon — "achha hoon."
Sach yaad nahin…
Aur hum jhoothe ban gaye.

Humne toh tay nahin kiya tha na hum kya hain,
Phir hum dekhte dekhte kya ban gaye?

Shayad yahi hota hoga har rishte mein —
Baatein kam ho jaati hongi,
Raatein mayoos ho jaati hongi,
Umr ke saath maathay par silvatein aa jaati hongi.

Shayad aakhir har rishte mein
Har baat
Sirf sawaal-jawaab ban jaati hogi.

ठीक हो?

"जी, ठीक हो?"
"हाँ, ठीक हूँ।"

"जी, खा लिया खाना?"
"हाँ जी, बस अभी।"

"जी, संभल के जाना।"
"जी, ज़रूर।"

पता नहीं कब हमारी बातें
यूँ सिर्फ सवाल-जवाब बन गईं।

अभी तो मिले ही थे ना –
दोस्त थे... और फिर अजनबी बन गए।

वो हाल पूछते हैं,
मैं कहता हूँ – "अच्छा हूँ।"
सच याद नहीं...
और हम झूठे बन गए।

हमने तो तय नहीं किया था ना हम क्या हैं,
फिर हम देखते-देखते क्या बन गए?

शायद यही होता होगा हर रिश्ते में –
बातें कम हो जाती होंगी,

रातें मायूस हो जाती होंगी,
उम्र के साथ माथे पर सिलवटें आ जाती होंगी।

शायद आखिर हर रिश्ते में
हर बात
सिर्फ सवाल-जवाब बन जाती होगी।

Khoya Toh Hai...

Aankh laal nahin toh kya — roya toh hai,
Woh mera tha hi nahin, par khoya toh hai.

Khoon ki boo se ghin na aa jaaye,
Likh kar khat maine ittar mein dooboya toh hai.

Na hunar koi, na kaam, na koi naukri,
Aate aur namak ka khwaab sanjhoya toh hai.

Mitti ka banaya, dhoop mein rakkha use,
Paani na mila toh tezaab mein bhigoya toh hai.

Muntazir — aakhir zehar hi likha tha naseeb mein,
Abhi do pal pehle hans ke soya toh hai.

खोया तो...

आँख लाल नहीं तो क्या – रोया तो है,
वो मेरा था ही नहीं, पर खोया तो है।

खून की बू से घिन न आ जाए,
लिख कर ख़त मैंने इत्तर में डुबोया तो है।

ना हुनर कोई, ना काम, ना कोई नौकरी,
आटे और नमक का ख़्वाब संजोया तो है।

मिट्टी का बनाया, धूप में रखा उसे,
पानी न मिला तो तेज़ाब में भिगोया तो है।

मुन्तज़िर – आखिर ज़हर ही लिखा था नसीब में,
अभी दो पल पहले हँस के सोया तो है।

Badal Gayi...

Jawaani mein aaya tha sheher kaam karne,
Jab gaon pahuncha — saari deewarein badal gayi.

Main jab tak lauta khud ko sudhaar kar,
Mere hum-numa ki saari shikaayatein badal gayi.

Woh uth ke jaane laga toh dil baith gaya mera,
Rukh yun moda usne — fizaayein badal gayi.

Main do-chaar din ishq mein mashroof raha,
Watan mein teen baar sarkaarein badal gayi.

Itni lambi thi sazaa ishq-e-zurm-e-judaai ki,
Qaid kaat-te kaat-te salakhein badal gayi.

Muntazir, main jaanta hoon kaun hai qaatil mera,
Muqaddama itna chala — dafaayein badal gayi.

बदल गईं...

जवानी में आया था शहर काम करने,
जब गाँव पहुँचा – सारी दीवारें बदल गईं।

मैं जब तक लौटा खुद को सुधार कर,
मेरे हमनुमा की सारी शिकायतें बदल गईं।

वो उठ के जाने लगा तो दिल बैठ गया मेरा,
रुख यूँ मोड़ा उसने – फ़िज़ाएँ बदल गईं।

मैं दो-चार दिन इश्क़ में मशरूफ़ रहा,
वतन में तीन बार सरकारें बदल गईं।

इतनी लंबी थी सज़ा इश्क़-ए-जुर्म-ए-जुदाई की,
क़ैद काटते-काटते सलाख़ें बदल गईं।

मुन्तज़िर, मैं जानता हूँ कौन है क़ातिल मेरा,
मुक़द्दमा इतना चला – दफ़ाएँ बदल गईं।

Kya Ban Gaya...

Kya banne nikla tha main ghar se — kya ban gaya,
Dekhte dekhte na jaane main kya se kya ban gaya.

Khwaab shuru hua toh haath mein tera haath tha,
Subah hote hote ye rishta anjaana ban gaya.

Ek duje ki dhadkan sunte the — yun paas the hum,
Ab chehra bhi yaad nahin — ye faasla kya ban gaya.

Chah kar bhi tujhse dil ki baat keh na paaya,
Tu hi padh le aankhon se — ye afsaana kya ban gaya.

Ishq ka ilm na tha toh zindagi qaabil-e-bardaasht thi,
Tere baad na jaane main sayana ya deewaana ban gaya.

क्या बन गया...

क्या बनने निकला था मैं घर से – क्या बन गया,
देखते-देखते न जाने मैं क्या से क्या बन गया।

ख़्वाब शुरू हुआ तो हाथ में तेरा हाथ था,
सुबह होते-होते ये रिश्ता अनजाना बन गया।

एक दूजे की धड़कन सुनते थे – यूँ पास थे हम,
अब चेहरा भी याद नहीं – ये फ़ासला क्या बन गया।

चाह कर भी तुझसे दिल की बात कह न पाया,
तू ही पढ़ ले आँखों से – ये अफ़साना क्या बन गया।

इश्क़ का इल्म न था तो ज़िंदगी क़ाबिल-ए-बर्दाश्त थी,
तेरे बाद न जाने मैं सयाना या दीवाना बन गया।

Pukarta Ho Koi...

Tere pyaar jaisa yakeen ho ya vehem ho koi,
Baar-baar jaise mera naam pukarta ho koi.

Main guzra us gali se — woh phir dikh gayi,
Kaleje mein garam loha jaise utarta ho koi.

Kisi ke paas zubaan ho, magar woh maun rahe,
Bhara jaam bas dekh kar hi madhosh ho koi.

Lagta hai kabhi koi toh sahaara ban jaaye,
Phir lagta hai — kaash mera kabhi na ho koi.

Ub gaya hoon khud se ab, kis-kis ko bataun,
Raah chalta haal-o-khabar poochta hai har koi.

Dekh, Muntazir — ye aakhri salaah hai,
Qayamat ho toh ho… par phir pyaar na ho koi.

पुकारता हो कोई...

तेरे प्यार जैसे यक़ीन हो या वहम हो कोई,
बार-बार जैसे मेरा नाम पुकारता हो कोई।

मैं गुज़रा उस गली से – वो फिर दिख गई,
कलेजे में गरम लोहा जैसे उतरता हो कोई।

किसी के पास ज़ुबान हो, मगर वो मौन रहे,
भरा जाम बस देख कर ही मदहोश हो कोई।

लगता है कभी कोई तो सहारा बन जाए,
फिर लगता है – काश मेरा कभी न हो कोई।

उब गया हूँ खुद से अब, किस-किस को बताऊँ,
राह चलता हाल-ओ-ख़बर पूछता है हर कोई।

देख, मुन्तज़िर – ये आख़िरी सलाह है,
क़यामत हो तो हो... पर फिर प्यार न हो कोई।

Mere Saare Apne...

Jab sunna hi na ho, toh kyun duhaai de,
Marne ki aas ho, toh phir kyun dawaai de?

Mere saare apne toh tune apne kar liye,
Mere haq se ab yahan kaun gawaahi de?

Darr lagta hai azaad ghoomne mein mujhe,
Mujhe meri hi qaid se ab kaun rihaai de?

Jaam khadakta hai toh jahaan sun leta hai,
Khaali dil ki goonj ab kaun sunai de?

Do pal ko hi sahi meri aankhen leke dekh,
Phir batana mujhe aaine mein jo dikhai de.

Maine kabhi tujhe bewafa samjha hi nahin,
Phir kyun jaa jaa ke gairon ko tu safaai de?

मेरे सारे अपने...

जब सुनना ही न हो, तो क्यों दुहाई दे,
मरने की आस हो, तो फिर क्यों दवाई दे?

मेरे सारे अपने तो तूने अपने कर लिए,
मेरे हक़ से अब यहाँ कौन गवाही दे?

डर लगता है आज़ाद घूमने में मुझे,
मुझे मेरी ही क़ैद से अब कौन रिहाई दे?

जाम खड़कता है तो जहाँ सुन लेता है,
खाली दिल की गूँज अब कौन सुनाई दे?

दो पल को ही सही मेरी आँखें लेकर देख,
फिर बताना मुझे आईने में जो दिखाई दे।

मैंने कभी तुझे बेवफ़ा समझा ही नहीं,
फिर क्यों जा-जा के ग़ैरों को तू सफ़ाई दे?

Suna Hai...

Suna hai tum mujhe milna chahte ho,
Kya phir se khoon-e-jigar rona chahte ho?

Ya dekh kar ishq-e-faqeer-e-haal mera,
Shayad tum chain se sona chahte ho?

Hamaara haath pakad kar hamaari kasamein khaayi,
Ab hamaare hi janaaze se muh modna chahte ho?

Suna hai tum mujhe milna chahte ho.

Toh aa jao phir usi jagah par,
Le aao saari shikaayat baandh kar.

Tum phir jeetna muqaddama,
Main gawaahi dunga,
Mita kar apne saare saboot,
Chala jaaunga main haar kar.

Phir se keh dena ek baar tum mujhe bewafa,
Sardi mein haath sek lena mere khat jala kar.

Aakhri baar le chalunga main bike par apni,
Rota hi sahi — chhod dunga tumhein ghar sambhaal kar.

Suna hai tum mujhe milna chahte ho,
Toote dil se na jaane ab aur kya chahte ho.

Suna hai tum mujhe milna chahte ho.

सुना है...

सुना है तुम मुझे मिलना चाहते हो,
क्या फिर से ख़ून-ए-जिगर रोना चाहते हो?

या देख कर इश्क़-ए-फ़क़ीर-ए-हाल मेरा,
शायद तुम चैन से सोना चाहते हो?

हमारा हाथ पकड़ कर हमारी क़समे खाई,
अब हमारे ही जनाज़े से मुँह मोड़ना चाहते हो?

सुना है तुम मुझे मिलना चाहते हो।

तो आ जाओ फिर उसी जगह पर,
ले आओ सारी शिकायत बाँध कर।

तुम फिर जीतना मुक़द्दमा – मैं गवाही दूँगा,
मिटा कर अपने सारे सबूत, चला जाऊँगा मैं हार कर।

फिर से कह देना एक बार तुम मुझे बेवफ़ा,
सर्दी में हाथ सेक लेना मेरे ख़त जला कर।

आख़िरी बार ले चलूँगा मैं बाइक पर अपनी,
रोता ही सही – छोड़ दूँगा तुम्हें घर संभाल कर।

सुना है तुम मुझे मिलना चाहते हो,
टूटे दिल से न जाने अब और क्या चाहते हो।

सुना है तुम मुझे मिलना चाहते हो।

Ghar Kar Lunga...

Dil behlane ko apna ab kis-kis ka dil main todunga,
Apne tutte dil mein hi main ek ghar kar lunga.

Kahaan banti hai ishq ke choolhe par pyaar ki roti,
Ab main daftar mein ghar, aur ghar ko daftar kar lunga.

Dil ka kya hai — us par marta jisse milti aankhen,
Saare fasaad ki jad hai — aankhon mein patthar bhar lunga.

Tumhein mubarak gulshan saare aur gulshan ke phool,
Kahin raat neend na aa jaaye — main sholon par bistar kar lunga.

Mumkin nahin bhoolna, par main tumko bhoolunga,
Na raha gaya toh chaand-taaron se tera zikr kar dunga.

Dil behlane ko apna ab kis-kis ka dil main todunga,
Apne tutte dil mein hi main ek ghar kar lunga.

घर कर लूँगा...

दिल बहलाने को अपना अब किस-किस का दिल मैं तोड़ूँगा,
अपने टूटे दिल में ही मैं एक घर कर लूँगा।

कहाँ बनती है इश्क़ के चूल्हे पर प्यार की रोटी,
अब मैं दफ़्तर में घर, और घर को दफ़्तर कर लूँगा।

दिल का क्या है – उस पर मरता जिससे मिलती आँखें,
सारे फ़साद की जड़ है – आँखों में पत्थर भर लूँगा।

तुम्हें मुबारक गुलशन सारे और गुलशन के फूल,
कहीं रात नींद न आ जाए – मैं शोलों पर बिस्तर कर लूँगा।

मुमकिन नहीं भूलना, पर मैं तुमको भूलूँगा,
ना रहा गया तो चाँद-तारों से तेरा ज़िक्र कर दूँगा।

दिल बहलाने को अपना अब किस-किस का दिल मैं तोड़ूँगा,
अपने टूटे दिल में ही मैं एक घर कर लूँगा।

Chaar Shaam...

Zindagi ki bachi hain chaar shaam,
Meri kitaabein, do gaane aur sasti sharaab.

Sota nahin ab — nashe mein behosh hota hoon,
Tu le ja apni yaad aur woh haseen khwaab.

Band kamre mein akele kaun teri yaad dilaye?
Khidki se chali hawa — aur dil hua betaab.

Hakeem pakde nabz — na marz, na ilaaj,
Dil khoon na aansu kheenche — bolo kya hai sabab?

Muntazir, mera toh naseeb hi yun likha hai,
Aaghaz hua bura — aur har anjaam kharaab.

चार शाम...

ज़िंदगी की बची हैं चार शाम,
मेरी किताबें, दो गाने और सस्ती शराब।

सोता नहीं अब – नशे में बेहोश होता हूँ,
तू ले जा अपनी याद और वो हसीन ख़्वाब।

बंद कमरे में अकेले कौन तेरी याद दिलाए?
खिड़की से चली हवा – और दिल हुआ बेताब।

हकीम पकड़े नब्ज़ – न मर्ज़, न इलाज,
दिल ख़ून न आँसू खींचे – बोलो क्या है सबब?

मुन्तज़िर, मेरा तो नसीब ही यूँ लिखा है,
आग़ाज़ हुआ बुरा – और हर अंजाम ख़राब।

ZINDA...

Abhi zinda hoon main — tu nabz toh dekh,
Maut ko tere intezaar mein intezaar par rakkha hai.

Tu le aa ek taraazu, rakh de jo bhi hai tera,
Maine tere saare khat aur pehla gulaab rakkha hai.

Tujhe jaldi thi bahut zindagi mein aage badhne ki,
Maine umeed aur waqt dono ko thaam kar rakkha hai.

Tune lagayi mehendi aur doli mein baith gayi,
Maine jaam, kitaab aur haath mein qalam rakkha hai.

Tu gair hai, apna hai, dost hai ya pyaar hai —
Chhodo… ab rishton ke naam mein kya rakkha hai.

Dekho, Muntazir — khud ko bhi zara dikhao,
Sirf bewafa hi kehte hain — "ishq mein kya rakkha hai."

ज़िंदा...

अभी ज़िंदा हूँ मैं – तू नब्ज़ तो देख,
मौत को तेरे इंतज़ार में इंतज़ार पर रखा है।

तू ले आ एक तराज़ू, रख दे जो भी है तेरा,
मैंने तेरे सारे ख़त और पहला गुलाब रखा है।

तुझे जल्दी थी बहुत ज़िंदगी में आगे बढ़ने की,
मैंने उम्मीद और वक़्त दोनों को थाम कर रखा है।

तूने लगाई मेहँदी और डोली में बैठ गई,
मैंने जाम, किताब और हाथ में क़लम रखा है।

तू ग़ैर है, अपना है, दोस्त है या प्यार है –
छोड़ो... अब रिश्तों के नाम में क्या रखा है।

देखो, मुन्तज़िर – ख़ुद को भी ज़रा दिखाओ,
सिर्फ़ बेवफ़ा ही कहते हैं – "इश्क़ में क्या रखा है।"

Dil Bhar Aaye...

Kaise na dil bhar aaye kisi ka,
Koi tujhe dekhe toh meri nazar se.

Sadqe jaaun main sau baar, sanam,
Teri har gham-o-taqleef mere sar se.

Khoon ya aansu — kuch toh baha tha,
Jab baji shehnai aur uthi thi doli tere ghar se.

Pukarta... par saath zamaana tha,
Chup raha teri rusvaai ke darr se.

Sharaben saari, saare nashe,
Rihaa na kar paaye tere pyaar ke asar se.

Doston se poochta hoon bahaane bana kar,
Mehroom nahin hoon teri kisi khabar se.

Mann nahin kaam mein — na kaam hai mann ka,
Phir bhi der se nikalta hoon aaj kal daftar se.

Gaur se dekh — mere maathe ke nishaan abhi hain,
Mera ek hissa aaj bhi pada hai tere dar se.

दिल भर आए...

कैसे न दिल भर आए किसी का,
कोई तुझे देखे तो मेरी नज़र से।

सदके जाऊँ मैं सौ बार, सनम,
तेरी हर ग़म-ओ-तकलीफ़ मेरे सर से।

ख़ून या आँसू – कुछ तो बहा था,
जब बजी शहनाई और उठी थी डोली तेरे घर से।

पुकारता... पर साथ ज़माना था,
चुप रहा तेरी रुसवाई के डर से।

शराबें सारी, सारे नशे,
रिहा न कर पाए तेरे प्यार के असर से।

दोस्तों से पूछता हूँ बहाने बना कर,
महरूम नहीं हूँ तेरी किसी ख़बर से।

मन नहीं काम में – न काम है मन का,
फिर भी देर से निकलता हूँ आजकल दफ़्तर से।

गौर से देख – मेरे माथे के निशान अभी हैं,
मेरा एक हिस्सा आज भी पड़ा है तेरे दर से।

Naam Mohabbat...

Tinka-tinka zinda jalna hai naam mohabbat,
Kacche dil ka khel nahi hai kaam mohabbat.

Nasha, suroor, behoshi, maut kya hai,
Aaghaz se anjaam tak piyo jaam mohabbat.

Chupke-ghutke darr-darr ke kya hai,
Karna hai toh karo sar-e-aam mohabbat.

Heer, Ranjha, Farhad aur Majnu kya hai,
Acche-acchon ko kar deti benaam mohabbat.

Aansu, tadap, dard aur sisak kya hai,
Aksar maut ke baad deti aaram mohabbat.

Wafa, jafa, vaadein, kasmein kya hai,
Jinhe na aati ho, wahi karte badnaam mohabbat.

Sona, chandi, heere, moti kya hai,
Khud ko bechkar chukani padti hai daam mohabbat.

नाम मोहब्बत...

तिनका-तिनका ज़िंदा जलना है नाम मोहब्बत,
कच्चे दिल का खेल नहीं है काम मोहब्बत।

नशा, सुरूर, बेहोशी, मौत क्या है,
आग़ाज़ से अंजाम तक पियो जाम मोहब्बत।

चुपके-घुटके, डर-डर के क्या है,
करना है तो करो सर-ए-आम मोहब्बत।

हीर, रांझा, फ़रहाद और मजनूँ क्या हैं,
अच्छे-अच्छों को कर देती बेनाम मोहब्बत।

आँसू, तड़प, दर्द और सिसक क्या है,
अक्सर मौत के बाद देती आराम मोहब्बत।

वफ़ा, जफ़ा, वादे, क़समें क्या हैं,
जिन्हें न आती हो, वही करते बदनाम मोहब्बत।

सोना, चाँदी, हीरे, मोती क्या हैं,
खुद को बेचकर चुकानी पड़ती है दाम मोहब्बत।

Ehsaan...

Bas ek baar milo, tumharein kuch ehsaan uttarne hai,
Vada tha, aasman se chaand taarein uttarne hai,

Apni kasamein de dekar tum ne milne bulaya hai,
Milte hi tumharein labbon pe jaane ke bahaane hai,

Tumhein laga tum joagi toh tanha ho jaunga main?
Mere jaise iss sheher main hazzaron deewane hai,

Main fakt ghar se bazaar kya gaya iss haalat main,
Dekho kitne log ghar aayein mujhe samjhaane hai,

Sheher ka naam se main ginn ke bata du main,
Kis Galli kis mod pe kitne maikhane hai,

Nazar aur nazariyan hi sab sahi galat kar deta hai,
Tumhein dekhu toh bahar, na dekhu toh veerane hai,

Waqt bewaqt bhi kabhi kabhi pee leni chahiye,
Bin wajah gaur karo todein kitne paimaane hai,

Tum puuch lo chahein jitna aur chahein jitni baar,
Mera dil ek tekhaane main aur uss main tehkaane hai,

एहसान...

बस एक बार मिलो, तुम्हारे कुछ एहसान उतारने हैं,
वादा था, आसमान से चाँद तारे उतारने हैं।

अपनी कसमें दे-देकर तुमने मिलने बुलाया है,
मिलते ही तुम्हारे लबों पे जाने के बहाने हैं।

तुम्हें लगा तुम जाओगी तो तन्हा हो जाऊँगा मैं?
मेरे जैसे इस शहर में हज़ारों दीवाने हैं।

मैं फ़क़्त घर से बाज़ार क्या गया इस हालत में,
देखो कितने लोग घर आए मुझे समझाने हैं।

शहर का नाम से मैं गिन के बता दूँ मैं,
किस गली, किस मोड़ पे कितने मयख़ाने हैं।

नज़र और नज़रिये ही सब सही-ग़लत कर देते हैं,
तुम्हें देखूँ तो बहार, न देखूँ तो वीराने हैं।

वक़्त-बेवक़्त भी कभी-कभी पी लेनी चाहिए,
बिन वजह गौर करो – टूटे कितने पैमाने हैं।

तुम पूछ लो चाहे जितना और चाहे जितनी बार,
मेरा दिल एक तहख़ाने में, और उसमें तहख़ाने हैं।

Kaash Aisa Ho Jayein...

Main kuch kahun,
Aur tu sharma jaaye.

Main kuch bolun,
Aur tu hans jaaye.

Baarish mein kadke bijli zor se,
Aur tu dhamm se darr jaaye.

Zor se pakde haath mera,
Aur seene se lag jaaye.

Raat kaatein baaton mein,
Aur subah chai peene jaayein.

Narm dhoop aaye khidki se,
Hum lipat kar so jaayein.

Ladein ki kaun zyada pyaar karta hai,
Phir bin kahe maan jaayein.

Zidd karein ki pehle tum khao,
Phir saath baith kar khaana khaayein.

Fikr kya ab jahaan duniya ki,
Tum se shuru aur wahin khatam ho jaaye.

Zalimaa, kaash aisa ho jaaye,
Toh zindagi kya se kya ho jaaye.

Ek umr kaat di tere dar par maine,
Sochta hoon ab ghar chala jaaye.

काश ऐसा हो जाए...

मैं कुछ कहूँ,
और तू शर्मा जाए।

मैं कुछ बोलूँ,
और तू हँस जाए।

बारिश में कड़के बिजली ज़ोर से,
और तू धम्म से डर जाए।

ज़ोर से पकड़े हाथ मेरा,
और सीने से लग जाए।

रात काटें बातों में,
और सुबह चाय पीने जाएँ।

नर्म धूप आए खिड़की से,
हम लिपट कर सो जाएँ।

लड़ें कि कौन ज़्यादा प्यार करता है,
फिर बिन कहे मान जाएँ।

ज़िद करें कि पहले तुम खाओ,
फिर साथ बैठकर खाना खाएँ।

फ़िक्र क्या अब जहाँ दुनिया की,
तुम से शुरू और वहीं ख़त्म हो जाए।

ज़ालिमा, काश ऐसा हो जाए,
तो ज़िंदगी क्या से क्या हो जाए।

एक उम्र काट दी तेरे दर पर मैंने,
सोचता हूँ अब घर चला जाए।

Baap...

Aawara parinda, kahin bhi ghar kar leta hain,
Geeli rait se sapnon ka ghar kar leta hain.

Saare jahaan ki khushi lekar bhi koi udaas hai,
Koi udaasi mein hans kar umr basar kar leta hain.

Kya museebat hai ki ab kisi ka saath gawara nahin,
Aata dost dekh kar woh raasta udhar kar leta hain.

Ji janaab, batao kya daleel hai, kya muqaddama hai,
Wo ro ke apne ishq ka ilzaam mere sar kar deta hain.

Kabhi ghar, toh khilone, ya roti, ya imarti ke liye,
Baap ek ek kar apne sapne kharch kar deta hai.

Chahu toh main bhi pahuch jau haath phailakar,
Suna hai maange pe wo sab pe karam kar deta hai.

बाप...

आवारा परिंदा कहीं भी घर कर लेता है,
गीली रेत से सपनों का घर कर लेता है।

सारे जहाँ की खुशी लेकर भी कोई उदास है,
कोई उदासी में हँसकर उम्र बसर कर लेता है।

क्या मुसीबत है कि अब किसी का साथ गवारा नहीं,
आता दोस्त देख कर वो रास्ता उधर कर लेता है।

जी जनाब, बताओ क्या दलील है, क्या मुक़द्दमा है,
वो रो के अपने इश्क़ का इल्ज़ाम मेरे सर कर देता है।

कभी घर, तो खिलौने, या रोटी, या इमरती के लिए,
बाप एक-एक कर अपने सपने खर्च कर देता है।

चाहूँ तो मैं भी पहुँच जाऊँ हाथ फैलाकर,
सुना है माँगे पे वो सब पे करम कर देता है।

Bas Itni Si Baat...

Mujhe ishq hai, tumhein nahi, bas itni si baat hai,
Tumhi ye aakar samjha do, bas itni si baat hai.

Maine sau baar likha tumhein khat mein pyaar,
Tum ek baar inkaar likh do, bas itni si baat hai.

Mujhe dekhte hi tumne parda kyun kar liya,
Aankh tumhari bhi sharmai to, bas itni si baat hai.

Log kehte hai main aur piyu toh mar jaaunga,
Tum pyaala apne haath se do, bas itni si baat hai.

Sirf pal do pal jo tum khidki pe dikh jao,
Meri akhri khwahish mita bhi do, bas itni si baat hai.

Main nahi maanta tum khuda ho, gar ho agar,
Uski baahein mere gale daal do, bas itni si baat hai.

Muntazir, maine kahan faansi se inkaar kiya hai,
Mera jurm koi bata toh do, bas itni si baat hai.

बस इतनी सी बात है...

मुझे इश्क़ है, तुम्हें नहीं – बस इतनी सी बात है,
तुम ही ये आकर समझा दो – बस इतनी सी बात है।

मैंने सौ बार लिखा तुम्हें ख़त में प्यार,
तुम एक बार इंकार लिख दो – बस इतनी सी बात है।

मुझे देखते ही तुमने पर्दा क्यों कर लिया,
आँख तुम्हारी भी शरमाई तो – बस इतनी सी बात है।

लोग कहते हैं मैं और पियूँ तो मर जाऊँगा,
तुम प्याला अपने हाथ से दो – बस इतनी सी बात है।

सिर्फ़ पल-दो-पल जो तुम खिड़की पे दिख जाओ,
मेरी आख़िरी ख़्वाहिश मिटा भी दो – बस इतनी सी बात है।

मैं नहीं मानता तुम ख़ुदा हो – गर हो अगर,
उसकी बाँहें मेरे गले डाल दो – बस इतनी सी बात है।

मुन्तज़िर, मैंने कहाँ फाँसी से इंकार किया है,
मेरा जुर्म कोई बता तो दो – बस इतनी सी बात है।

Ishq इश्क़

Ishq mein haar, jeet, nafa-nuksaan kahan hota hai,

Ishq ka hona hi bahut hai — ishq bas hona hota hai.

इश्क़ में हार, जीत, नफ़ा-नुक़सान कहाँ होता है,

इश्क़ का होना ही बहुत है – इश्क़ बस होना होता है।

KHWAAB...

Tum baitho mere paas jo aakar,
Aur bol do mera naam,
Teri aankhon ko sapna likhu,
Raat likhu,
Ya likhu main jaam.

Tu kas ke gale lagaye mujhe,
Aur sab gham bhool jaaun,
Teri baahon ko main ghar likhu,
Darr likhu,
Ya likhu main aaraam.

Kandhe par sir rakh soye tu,
Kaano mein ho bas teri saansein,
Isko main khwahish likhu,
Armaan likhu,
Ya likhu main khwaab.

ख़्वाब...

तुम बैठो मेरे पास जो आकर,
और बोल दो मेरा नाम,
तेरी आँखों को सपना लिखूँ,
रात लिखूँ,
या लिखूँ मैं जाम।

तू कस के गले लगाए मुझे,
और सब ग़म भूल जाऊँ,
तेरी बाँहों को मैं घर लिखूँ,
डर लिखूँ,
या लिखूँ मैं आराम।

कंधे पर सिर रख सोए तू,
कानों में हो बस तेरी साँसें,
इसको मैं ख़्वाहिश लिखूँ,
अरमान लिखूँ,
या लिखूँ मैं ख़्वाब।

Pighal Jaati Hai...

Use lagta hai woh bahut sakht, sang-e-khisht si hai,
Sir se paa tak mom hai, maatha chummon toh pighal jaati hai.

Use lagta hai woh chalaak, sayyani aur tez hai bahut,
Par use duniya-duniyadaari kahaan samajh aati hai.

Khud hi apna dil lekar khud hi bech deti hai,
Kya karein, masoom ko kahaan kharidaari samajh aati hai.

Use lagta uska gham sirf uska hai, kyun kisi ko bole,
Aur kisi aur ka dard dekh kar aansu-aansu ho jaati hai.

Hum mile bhi us mod par jab kandhon par bojh bahut tha,
"Hum humsafar nahi, fakt dost hain" — ye mujhe rote-rote samjhaati hai.

Mujh se kaafir ko bhi unhone khuda-parast bana diya,
Jab tak na namaaz padh loon, woh paagal khana nahi khaati.

Pal mein hansna, pal mein rona — uff hai mizaaj uska,
Pal-pal baat badal de, jaise titli phoolon se udd jaati hai.

Barson nahi milti, par jab bhi milne woh aati hai,
Milti hai mujhe jaise nadiyaan saagar mein mil jaati hain.

Aasaani se padh leti hai woh Momin, Rumi aur Ghalib ko,
Main tareef karoon toh kehti — "Urdu samajh nahi aati."

पिघल जाती है...

उसे लगता है वो बहुत सख़्त, संग-ए-ख़िश्त सी है,
सिर से पाँव तक मोम है, माथा चूमूँ तो पिघल जाती है।

उसे लगता है वो चालाक, सय्यानी और तेज़ है बहुत,
पर उसे दुनिया-दुनियादारी कहाँ समझ आती है।

ख़ुद ही अपना दिल लेकर ख़ुद ही बेच देती है,
क्या करें, मासूम को कहाँ ख़रीदारी समझ आती है।

उसे लगता उसका ग़म सिर्फ उसका है, क्यों किसी को बोले,
और किसी और का दर्द देख कर आँसू-आँसू हो जाती है।

हम मिले भी उस मोड़ पर जब कंधों पर बोझ बहुत था,
"हम हमसफ़र नहीं, फ़क़्त दोस्त हैं" – ये मुझे रोते-रोते समझाती है।

मुझ से काफ़िर को भी उन्होंने ख़ुदा-परस्त बना दिया,
जब तक न नमाज़ पढ़ लूँ, वो पागल खाना नहीं खाती।

पल में हँसना, पल में रोना – उफ़ है मिज़ाज उसका,
पल-पल बात बदल दे, जैसे तितली फूलों से उड़ जाती है।

बरसों नहीं मिलती, पर जब भी मिलने वो आती है,
मिलती है मुझे जैसे नदियाँ सागर में मिल जाती हैं।

आसानी से पढ़ लेती है वो मोमिन, रूमी और ग़ालिब को,
मैं तारीफ़ करूँ तो कहती – "उर्दू समझ नहीं आती है।"

Bilkul Nahi...

Mujhe chahiye duniya saari,
Tu poora mil — ya bilkul nahin.

Main pee loon maikhana saara,
Tu pyaala, tu saaqi — ya bilkul nahin.

Kalma, sajda, imaan kis ke liye?
Hai khuda toh mile — ya bilkul nahin.

Naraaz hai woh humse itna kyun?
Ya bahut hai pyaar — ya bilkul nahin.

Ya keh do apna, ya phir begaana,
Sach bol do, sanam — itna bhi mushkil nahin.

बिल्कुल नहीं...

मुझे चाहिए दुनिया सारी,
तू पूरा मिल – या बिल्कुल नहीं।

मैं पी लूँ मयख़ाना सारा,
तू प्याला, तू साक़ी – या बिल्कुल नहीं।

कलमा, सजदा, ईमान किस के लिए?
है ख़ुदा तो मिले – या बिल्कुल नहीं।

नाराज़ है वो हमसे इतना क्यों?
या बहुत है प्यार – या बिल्कुल नहीं।

या कह दो अपना, या फिर बेगाना,
सच बोल दो, सनम – इतना भी मुश्किल नहीं।

GUFTAGU...

Shaam-e-gham kehta hai Muntazir se...

Ae dil-e-muntazir, kya haal bana liya hai,
Kyun us ek shakhs ko saara jahaan bana liya hai.

Ae dil-e-muntazir, kya jalne se nahi darta?
Kyun khud ko parwana aur usko shamaa bana liya hai.

Ae dil-e-muntazir, ab kyun gaahe-gaahe rota hai,
Jo tere dil se anjaan hai — use hi jaan bana liya hai.

Ae dil-e-muntazir, masjid mein baitha hai na tu,
Phir us kaafir ko khuda aur imaan bana liya hai.

Ae dil-e-muntazir, ek-tarfa pyaar nahi achha,
Phir kyun zid karke unki naa ko haan bana liya hai.

Muntazir farmaata hai...

Ae shaam-e-gham, tu kyun dekhe haal mera,
Kyun aitraaz hai tujhe — jo maine use apna jahaan bana liya hai?

Ae shaam-e-gham, kya baaqi hai ab jalne ko,
Jalte hum dono hi hain — kya fark kisne shamaa, kisne parwana bana liya hai?

Ae shaam-e-gham, kyun aansuon ka hisaab kare,
Kyun ishq ko karobaar aur dil ko bahi-khaata bana liya hai?

Ae shaam-e-gham, main masjid toh kabhi gaya nahi,
Tu dhoondta reh gaya khuda — maine unko khuda bana liya hai.

Ae shaam-e-gham, jaan le — pyaar mein taraf aur kona nahi,
Ek-tarfa mohabbat karke khud ko aadam se insaan bana liya hai.

गुफ़्तगू

शाम-ए-ग़म कहता है मुन्तज़िर से...

ऐ दिल-ए-मुन्तज़िर, क्या हाल बना लिया है,
क्यों उस एक शख़्स को सारा जहाँ बना लिया है।

ऐ दिल-ए-मुन्तज़िर, क्या जलने से नहीं डरता?
क्यों ख़ुद को परवाना और उसको शमा बना लिया है।

ऐ दिल-ए-मुन्तज़िर, अब क्यों गाहे-गाहे रोता है,
जो तेरे दिल से अनजान है – उसे ही जान बना लिया है।

ऐ दिल-ए-मुन्तज़िर, मस्जिद में बैठा है न तू,
फिर उस काफ़िर को ख़ुदा और ईमान बना लिया है।

ऐ दिल-ए-मुन्तज़िर, एक-तरफ़ा प्यार नहीं अच्छा,
फिर क्यों ज़िद करके उनकी ना को हाँ बना लिया है।

मुन्तज़िर फ़रमाता है...

ऐ शाम-ए-ग़म, तू क्यों देखे हाल मेरा,
क्यों ऐतराज़ है तुझे – जो मैंने उसे अपना जहाँ बना लिया है?

ऐ शाम-ए-ग़म, क्या बाक़ी है अब जलने को,
जलते हम दोनों ही हैं – क्या फ़र्क किसने शमा, किसने परवाना बना लिया है?

ऐ शाम-ए-ग़म, क्यों आँसुओं का हिसाब करे,
क्यों इश्क़ को कारोबार और दिल को बही-ख़ाता बना लिया है?

ऐ शाम-ए-ग़म, मैं मस्जिद तो कभी गया नहीं,
तू ढूँढ़ता रह गया ख़ुदा – मैंने उनको ख़ुदा बना लिया है।

ऐ शाम-ए-ग़म, जान ले – प्यार में तरफ़ और कोना नहीं,
एक-तरफ़ा मोहब्बत करके ख़ुद को आदम से इंसान बना लिया है।

Himmat Rakhte Hai...

Beintihaa mohabbat karke bhi,
Pal mein bhoolne ki himmat rakhte hain.

Khudi ko raakh karke bhi,
Sholon par chalne ki himmat rakhte hain.

Faqeer hai haalat meri phir bhi,
Tere naam ki daawat rakhte hain.

Masjid, kalma, sajda kya hai,
Hum sirf aap ki ibaadat rakhte hain.

Bas ek baar kabhi izhaar kyun nahi karte?
Ek-tarfa pyaar se bas itni shikayat rakhte hain.

हिम्मत रखते हैं...

बेइंतिहा मोहब्बत करके भी,
पल में भूलने की हिम्मत रखते हैं।

ख़ुदी को राख करके भी,
शोलों पर चलने की हिम्मत रखते हैं।

फ़क़ीर है हालत मेरी फिर भी,
तेरे नाम की दावत रखते हैं।

मस्जिद, कलमा, सजदा क्या है,
हम सिर्फ़ आप की इबादत रखते हैं।

बस एक बार कभी इज़हार क्यों नहीं करते?
एक-तरफ़ा प्यार से बस इतनी शिकायत रखते हैं।

Ishq Hai Aatish...

Ishq hai aatish, Ghalib — is par zor chalta nahin,
Humein hai, usse nahin — is par zor chalta nahin.

Maine unhe bhi chup-chup rote dekha hai magar,
Mom sa hai dil unka — ya patthar jo pighalta nahin.

Sirf chai, sutta aur sharaab se guzaara hai,
Unse milne ko main ghar se nikalta nahin.

Pehli baar dekha tha — kaali bindi aur kurta laal,
Tab sirf usi mein khuda dikha — kahin aur ab khuda dikhta nahin.

Mar gaye gulaab saare aur kitaabein phat gayin,
Ek teri tasveer chhod — main kamra bhi saaf karta nahin.

Kyun dhong rachaaya yaari, wafa aur pyaar ka,
Marz-e-maut ka bhi ilaaj mil jaata hai,
Bas ishq ka ilaaj milta nahin.

इश्क़ है आतिश...

इश्क़ है आतिश, ग़ालिब – इस पर ज़ोर चलता नहीं,
हमें है, उसे नहीं – इस पर ज़ोर चलता नहीं।

मैंने उन्हें भी चुप-चुप रोते देखा है मगर,
मोम सा है दिल उनका – या पत्थर जो पिघलता नहीं।

सिर्फ़ चाय, सिगरेट और शराब से गुज़ारा है,
उनसे मिलने को मैं घर से निकलता नहीं।

पहली बार देखा था – काली बिंदी और कुर्ता लाल,
तब सिर्फ़ उसी में ख़ुदा दिखा – कहीं और अब ख़ुदा दिखता नहीं।

मर गए गुलाब सारे और किताबें फट गईं,
एक तेरी तस्वीर छोड़ – मैं कमरा भी साफ़ करता नहीं।

क्यों ढोंग रचाया यारी, वफ़ा और प्यार का,
मर्ज़-ए-मौत का भी इलाज मिल जाता है,
बस इश्क़ का इलाज मिलता नहीं।

Aapne Likha Hai?...

Woh poochhe ki ji, ye sher aapne likha hai?
Khayal unke hain, par haan — ye sher maine likha hai.

Maathe ki silvaton aur haathon ki lakeeron mein,
Koi toh padh ke batao ki kismat mein kya likha hai.

Aur kya kehna, aur kitni shikayatein baaqi hain,
Dekho na, khat mein kya kuch achha likha hai.

Nichod ke dekho toh kya abhi kuch baaqi hai,
Aadha khoon aur aadha siyaahi se likha hai.

Sher toh sher hai — us mein itna kya hai?
Ya sachchai hai, ya koi fasaana likha hai.

Haan, Muntazir, jaante ho tum unki chahat ko,
Par woh bhi tumhein hi chahein — ye kahaan likha hai?

Woh poochhe ki ji, ye sher aapne likha hai?
Khayal unke hain, par haan — ye sher maine likha hai.

आपने लिखा है...

वो पूछे कि जी, ये शेर आपने लिखा है?
ख़याल उनके हैं, पर हाँ – ये शेर मैंने लिखा है।

माथे की सिलवटों और हाथों की लकीरों में,
कोई तो पढ़ के बताओ कि क़िस्मत में क्या लिखा है।

और क्या कहना, और कितनी शिकायतें बाक़ी हैं,
देखो न, ख़त में क्या कुछ अच्छा लिखा है।

निचोड़ के देखो तो क्या अभी कुछ बाक़ी है,
आधा ख़ून और आधा सियाही से लिखा है।

शेर तो शेर है – उस में इतना क्या है?
या सच्चाई है, या कोई फ़साना लिखा है।

हाँ, मुन्तज़िर, जानते हो तुम उनकी चाहत को,
पर वो भी तुम्हें ही चाहें – ये कहाँ लिखा है?

वो पूछे कि जी, ये शेर आपने लिखा है?
ख़याल उनके हैं, पर हाँ – ये शेर मैंने लिखा है।

Tu Gayi Toh...

Tu gayi toh kalam se siyahi chali gayi,
Qaid bhi na mili aur rihaayi chali gayi.

Main toh baitha tha tabaah hone ke liye,
Haal mera dekh — tabaahi bhi chali gayi.

Saare doston ko bulaya kasamein de de kar,
Tera ek aansu gira, aur udhar saari gawaahi chali gayi.

Phir kaha maine — ab tum hi faisla karo,
Umr beet gayi sharaab mein, aur sunwaai chali gayi.

Pyaar mera sachcha tha ya khuda jaane,
Rusva jisne bhi kiya, uski khudai chali gayi.

Woh ro diye sunkar — Muntazir ne zubaan kaat li,
Khamosh ho gayi fariyaad, aur chup hi duhaai ho gayi.

तू गई तो...

तू गई तो क़लम से सियाही चली गई,
क़ैद भी न मिली और रिहाई चली गई।

मैं तो बैठा था तबाह होने के लिए,
हाल मेरा देख – तबाही भी चली गई।

सारे दोस्तों को बुलाया क़समे दे-दे कर,
तेरा एक आँसू गिरा, और उधर सारी गवाही चली गई।

फिर कहा मैंने – अब तुम ही फ़ैसला करो,
उम्र बीत गई शराब में, और सुनवाई चली गई।

प्यार मेरा सच्चा था या ख़ुदा जाने,
रुसवा जिसने भी किया, उसकी ख़ुदाई चली गई।

वो रो दिए सुनकर – मुन्तज़िर ने ज़ुबान काट ली,
ख़ामोश हो गई फ़रियाद, और चुप ही दुहाई हो गई।

Ye Aakhri Khat...

Lo mera aakhri khat padh lo,
Na hogi meri khabar, na sataane ko koi fikr.

Baat na hogi apni, na hoga ishq ka zikr,
Bahane sun liye saare — sun liye sab agar-magar

Anjaan banna tum dekh kar,
Ban jaaunga main bekhabar

Lo, ab aakhri hai — ye khat padh lo

Bhej di wapas woh kitaab, bata do kuch baaqi ho hisaab,
Hakeem ne tod di umeed meri — jiyoge saalon, tabiyat nahi kharaab

Main — ek kamra, ek khaali almaari,
Is mein tere jhooth aur fareb ki bharmaar

Dekho, nahi poocha maine kahin,
Kyun hai ye sawaal, aur kahan hai woh jawaab

Bas mere liye ek aakhri baar padh lo

Woh phool the na — murjha gaye
Woh panchhi the na — ghabra gaye
Woh taare the na — bujh gaye

Woh baatein thi na — hum dafn kar gaye
Woh raatein thi na — hum subah kar gaye

Umeed hai padha hoga,
Meri aakhri mohabbat ka,
Ye aakhri khat

ये आख़िरी ख़त...

लो मेरा आख़िरी ख़त पढ़ लो,
न होगी मेरी ख़बर, न सताने को कोई फ़िक्र।

बात न होगी अपनी, न होगा इश्क़ का ज़िक्र,
बहाने सुन लिए सारे – सुन लिए सब अगर-मगर।

अनजान बनना तुम देख कर,
बन जाऊँगा मैं बेख़बर।

लो, अब आख़िरी है – ये ख़त पढ़ लो।

भेज दी वापस वो किताब, बता दो कुछ बाक़ी हो हिसाब,
हकीम ने तोड़ दी उम्मीद मेरी – जियोगे सालों, तबियत नहीं ख़राब।

मैं – एक कमरा, एक खाली अलमारी,
इस में तेरे झूठ और फ़रेब की भरमार।

देखो, नहीं पूछा मैंने कहीं,
क्यों है ये सवाल, और कहाँ है वो जवाब।

बस मेरे लिए एक आख़िरी बार पढ़ लो।

वो फूल थे न – मुरझा गए।
वो पंछी थे न – घबरा गए।
वो तारे थे न – बुझ गए।
वो बातें थीं न – हम दफ़्न कर गए।
वो रातें थीं न – हम सुबह कर गए।

उम्मीद है पढ़ा होगा,
मेरी आख़िरी मोहब्बत का,
ये आख़िरी ख़त।

Kya Karu...

Main toh chahta hoon ki faqat shayari karun,
Kaun bewakoof chahta hai ki faqat naukri karun?

Khushnaseeb hain Faiz, Firaq, Jaun aur Momin,
Mujhe itni ijaazat nahin ki yun awaargi karun.

Kuch main na-samajh hoon, kuch woh haseen hai,
Unse hi shikaayat hai — unki hi tarafdaari karun.

Momin, tu bata — tu toh Allah ko jaanta hai na?
Khuda se, yaar se, raqib se — main kiski wafadaari karun?

Muntazir, tu hi bata — ye koi acchi baat hai?
Main khud deewana ho gaya — kya unhein bhi deewani karun?

क्या करूँ...

मैं तो चाहता हूँ कि फ़क़त शायरी करूँ,
कौन बेवक़ूफ़ चाहता है कि फ़क़त नौकरी करूँ?

ख़ुशनसीब हैं फ़ैज़, फ़िराक़, जौन और मोमिन,
मुझे इतनी इजाज़त नहीं कि यूँ आवारगी करूँ।

कुछ मैं नासमझ हूँ, कुछ वो हसीन है,
उनसे ही शिकायत है – उनकी ही तरफ़दारी करूँ।

मोमिन, तू बता – तू तो अल्लाह को जानता है न?
ख़ुदा से, यार से, रक़ीब से – मैं किसकी वफ़ादारी करूँ?

मुन्तज़िर, तू ही बता – ये कोई अच्छी बात है?
मैं ख़ुद दीवाना हो गया – क्या उन्हें भी दीवानी करूँ?

Kisse...

Aa sunaun tumhein jhoothi mohabbat ke kisse,
Fareb se bhare, banawati pyaar ke kisse.

Naqli log hain — naqli dil se pyaar karein,
Suno ab bewajah takraar ke kisse.

Pehle zikr hua, phir fikr, phir yaad — phir bhool gaye,
Mujhe bewafa likhen jab bhi likhen pyaar ke kisse.

Na shagird mila, na kalam, na kaagaz,
Koi sahi alfaaz sikhata toh likhte hum bhi pyaar ke kisse.

Tu bhi chala mere dar se — shaam ho chuki,
Mayusi aur khaali-pan — mere hi tarafdaar ke kisse.

Muntazir, tum ho jo mujhe achha maan baitho ho,
Kabhi unke muh se suno mere kirdaar ke kisse.

किस्से...

आ सुनाऊँ तुम्हें झूठी मोहब्बत के किस्से,
फ़रेब से भरे, बनावटी प्यार के किस्से।

नक़ली लोग हैं – नक़ली दिल से प्यार करें,
सुनो अब बेवजह तकरार के किस्से।

पहले ज़िक्र हुआ, फिर फ़िक्र, फिर याद – फिर भूल गए,
मुझे बेवफ़ा लिखें जब भी लिखें प्यार के किस्से।

न शागिर्द मिला, न क़लम, न काग़ज़,
कोई सही अल्फ़ाज़ सिखाता तो लिखते हम भी प्यार के किस्से।

तू भी चला मेरे दर से – शाम हो चुकी,
मायूसी और खालीपन – मेरे ही तरफ़दार के किस्से।

मुन्तज़िर, तुम हो जो मुझे अच्छा मान बैठे हो,
कभी उनके मुँह से सुनो मेरे किरदार के किस्से।

Jiya Karo...

Meri fikr, yaara, itni na kiya karo,
Mere bache hain chaar din — tum apni zindagi jiya karo.

Milaawat toh ab rooh aur imaan mein hai,
Jo bhi de koi pyaala — dekh kar piya karo.

Ameer niklein jo nange bhi toh kisi ko aitraaz na hoga,
Jo gareeb ho, toh phata daaman sambhaal kar siya karo.

Bhar jaaunga main pyaala-o-sagar sa,
Mujhe itna pyaar haule se diya karo.

Zamaane ki sunne lagein toh saans bhi na lene degi,
Thodi baghaavat karo — thoda baaghi hokar jiya karo.

Ek dil mein apne aur kitne qaid karoge?
Ya toh meri sunwaai karo, ya phir rihaa karo.

जिया करो...

मेरी फ़िक्र, यारा, इतनी न किया करो,
मेरे बचे हैं चार दिन – तुम अपनी ज़िंदगी जिया करो।

मिलावट तो अब रूह और ईमान में है,
जो भी दे कोई प्याला – देख कर पिया करो।

अमीर निकलें जो नंगे भी तो किसी को एतराज़ न होगा,
जो ग़रीब हो, तो फटा दामन संभाल कर सिया करो।

भर जाऊँगा मैं प्याला-ओ-सागर सा,
मुझे इतना प्यार हौले से दिया करो।

ज़माने की सुनने लगें तो साँस भी न लेने देगी,
थोड़ी बग़ावत करो – थोड़ा बाग़ी होकर जिया करो।

एक दिल में अपने और कितने क़ैद करोगे?
या तो मेरी सुनवाई करो, या फिर रिहा करो।

Qabool Kar Dein...

Har dua qabool kar dein,
Hum aise farishton ko bhi jaante hain.

Na uljhe ho aur jo na toote,
Hum aise rishton ko bhi jaante hain.

Jhoothi kasam khaayein jo har baat par,
Hum aise sachchon ko bhi jaante hain.

Manzilein dikhegi saari saraab mein,
Hum aise raaston ko bhi jaante hain.

Daava yaari ka, par daaman mein khanjar,
Hum aise doston ko bhi jaante hain.

Pyaar ka zeher bhi pal mein utaar de,
Hum aise arq-o-sharbat bhi jaante hain.

Ab rehne do, tumhein aur kya bataayein,
Hum aap ke baare jo bhi jaante hain.

क़बूल कर दें...

हर दुआ क़बूल कर दें,
हम ऐसे फ़रिश्तों को भी जानते हैं।

न उलझे हों और जो न टूटे,
हम ऐसे रिश्तों को भी जानते हैं।

झूठी क़सम खाएँ जो हर बात पर,
हम ऐसे सच्चों को भी जानते हैं।

मंज़िलें दिखेंगी सारी सराब में,
हम ऐसे रास्तों को भी जानते हैं।

दावा यारी का, पर दामन में ख़ंजर,
हम ऐसे दोस्तों को भी जानते हैं।

प्यार का ज़हर भी पल में उतार दे,
हम ऐसे अर्क़-ओ-शरबत भी जानते हैं।

अब रहने दो, तुम्हें और क्या बताएं,
हम आप के बारे जो भी जानते हैं।

SUKOON सुकून

Main sukoon yaar-e-daaman main dhoondta raha,

Sukoon mujhe farz-e-insaan main dhoondta raha,

मैं सुकून यार-ए-दामन में ढूँढ़ता रहा,

सुकून मुझे फ़र्ज़-ए-इंसान में ढूँढ़ता रहा।

Rahgir...

Yun mayoos na ho raahgir, ki rahein aur bhi hain,
Khwaahishein aur kar, ki manzilein aur bhi hain.

Kyun rota hai jo woh kissa adhoora reh gaya,
Koi nayi kahani likh, ki silsile aur bhi hain.

Mausam hi tha kuch aisa ki phool murjha gaye,
Barsaat ki umeed na chhod, ki bahaarein aur bhi hain.

Geela daaman kab tak aansuon se bhigota rahe,
Khuda ka shukr mana, ki jeene ke sahaare aur bhi hain.

Kyun rota hai ki unka daaman koi uda le gaya,
Tu apni mutthi khol ke dekh, ki hawayein aur bhi hain.

Baar-baar wahi harf-o-gham kyun padhte rehte ho,
Uthao Meer-o-Faraz-o-Rumi, ki kitaabein aur bhi hain.

राहगीर...

यूँ मायूस न हो राहगीर, कि राहें और भी हैं,
ख़्वाहिशें और कर, कि मंज़िलें और भी हैं।

क्यों रोता है जो वो क़िस्सा अधूरा रह गया,
कोई नई कहानी लिख, कि सिलसिले और भी हैं।

मौसम ही था कुछ ऐसा कि फूल मुरझा गए,
बरसात की उम्मीद न छोड़, कि बहारें और भी हैं।

गीला दामन कब तक आँसुओं से भिगोता रहे,
ख़ुदा का शुक्र मना, कि जीने के सहारे और भी हैं।

क्यों रोता है कि उनका दामन कोई उड़ा ले गया,
तू अपनी मुट्ठी खोल के देख, कि हवाएँ और भी हैं।

बार-बार वही हरफ़-ओ-ग़म क्यों पढ़ते रहते हो,
उठाओ मीर-ओ-फ़राज़-ओ-रूमी, कि किताबें और भी हैं।

Salaam-Dua...

Na vaid, hakeem, na peer — na koi dawa hai,
Raahat is marz ki sirf teri salaam-duaa hai.

Main maare-maare phirun unka naam lete hue,
Woh poochte hain iss baar mujhe kis se ishq hua hai?

Jal rahi hai ishq mein ab raakh bhi meri,
Woh poochte hain — aag kahaan hai, aur kahaan dhuan hai?

Apnon ko dekha apnon ka nivaala chheen,
Chhed mein thaali hai ab toh — ye kaisa jahaan hai?

Dekh toh meri aankhon mein kitni fariyaadein hain,
But ban gaya kya tu — tu kaisa khuda hai?

Jaane do yaar, ab kis-kis ka gham manayein,
Kaun rahega saath, aur peeche kya chhuta hai.

सलाम-दुआ

न वैद, हकीम, न पीर – न कोई दवा है,
राहत इस मर्ज़ की सिर्फ़ तेरी सलाम-दुआ है।

मैं मारे-मारे फिरूँ उनका नाम लेते हुए,
वो पूछते हैं इस बार मुझे किस से इश्क़ हुआ है?

जल रही है इश्क़ में अब राख भी मेरी,
वो पूछते हैं – आग कहाँ है, और कहाँ धुआँ है?

अपनों को देखा अपनों का निवाला छीन,
छेद में थाली है अब तो – ये कैसा जहाँ है?

देख तो मेरी आँखों में कितनी फरियादें हैं,
बुत बन गया क्या तू – तू कैसा ख़ुदा है?

जाने दो यार, अब किस-किस का ग़म मनाएँ,
कौन रहेगा साथ, और पीछे क्या छूटा है।

Zaroor...

Main bharam rakh bhi loon,
Khwaab toh khwaab hai — tootega zaroor.

Javedaani ka qarar Heer-Ranjha mein bhi tha,
Saath toh saath hai — chhootega zaroor.

Main patthar kar bhi loon dil magar,
Woh muskuraayen jo ek baar — pighlega zaroor.

Jo koodne se pehle hi darr gaya,
Khuda bhi bachaane aaye — doobega zaroor.

Aaj bhale lage ki kabhi na rukega,
Dard toh dard hai — rukega zaroor.

Umr bhar bhi na mila jo sukoon dil ko,
Tu leta reh unka naam — milega zaroor.

Muntazir, yun na chalo masjid mein akad kar,
Sar toh sar hai — jhukega zaroor.

ज़रूर...

मैं भरम रख भी लूँ,
ख़्वाब तो ख़्वाब है – टूटेगा ज़रूर।

जावेदानी का क़रार हीर-रांझा में भी था,
साथ तो साथ है – छूटेगा ज़रूर।

मैं पत्थर कर भी लूँ दिल मगर,
वो मुस्कुराएँ जो एक बार – पिघलेगा ज़रूर।

जो कूदने से पहले ही डर गया,
ख़ुदा भी बचाने आए – डूबेगा ज़रूर।

आज भले लगे कि कभी न रुकेगा,
दर्द तो दर्द है – रुकेगा ज़रूर।

उम्र भर भी न मिला जो सुकून दिल को,
तू लेता रह उनका नाम – मिलेगा ज़रूर।

मुन्तज़िर, यूँ न चलो मस्जिद में अकड़ कर,
सर तो सर है – झुकेगा ज़रूर।

Haal Mera...

Dil bezaar hai kyun itna, kya dekhe haal mera,
Tu apni bata yaar — accha hai haal mera.

Dekh toh dil apne, kuch toh haan hoga,
Saaf inkaar kar dete ho, chahe jo ho sawaal mera.

Ji nahin, ab cigarette aur sharaab chhod di,
Aapko vaada diya hai — main rakhunga khayaal mera.

Main jaaunga toh aankhon ki raunak le jaaunga,
Chaand, taare, roshni — tu dekhna kamaal mera.

Kiya bahut ishq haseenon, kitaabon aur fakiron se,
Ho gaya sab ka hisaab — ab Khuda se hai visaal mera.

Muntazir kal raat ko intiqaal farma gaya,
Khat mein toh likha tha — accha hai haal uska.

हाल मेरा...

दिल बेज़ार है क्यों इतना, क्या देखे हाल मेरा,
तू अपनी बता यार – अच्छा है हाल मेरा।

देख तो दिल अपने, कुछ तो हाँ होगा,
क्यों इंकार कर देते हो, चाहे जो भी सवाल मेरा।

जी नहीं, अब सिगरेट और शराब छोड़ दी,
आपको वादा दिया है – मैं रखूँगा ख़याल मेरा।

मैं जाऊँगा तो आँखों की रौनक ले जाऊँगा,
चाँद, तारे, रोशनी – तू देखना कमाल मेरा।

किया बहुत इश्क़ हसीनों, किताबों और फ़क़ीरों से,
हो गया सब का हिसाब – अब ख़ुदा से है विसाल मेरा।

मुन्तज़िर कल रात को इंतिक़ाल फ़रमा गया,
ख़त में तो लिखा था – अच्छा है हाल उसका।

Aakhri Jaam Hai...

Saaqi ab sharam na kar, ye aakhri jaam hai,
Chahe zeher hi de de mujhe — ye aakhri jaam hai.

Sultanat-o-daulat-o-shauhrat ki kya fikr karun,
Mujhe fikr hai raat kat jaaye — ye aakhri jaam hai.

Tu bhi khaali haath lauta maikhaane se,
La pyaala — us mein khoon bharun, ye aakhri jaam hai.

Bura kaho chahe bhala kaho tum mujhe ab,
Bas batao kahaan sharaab hai — ye aakhri jaam hai.

Kasam tumhari mehfil mein phir na aaunga,
Ab aur unki baatein na karo — ye aakhri jaam hai.

Kaun jaane kya jannat hai, kya hai dozakh,
Tu sharaab-e-rang-o-khushboo dekh — ye aakhri jaam hai.

आख़िरी जाम है...

साक़ी अब शर्म न कर, ये आख़िरी जाम है,
चाहे ज़हर ही दे दे मुझे – ये आख़िरी जाम है।

सुल्तनत-ओ-दौलत-ओ-शौहरत की क्या फ़िक्र करूँ,
मुझे फ़िक्र है रात कट जाए – ये आख़िरी जाम है।

तू भी खाली हाथ लौटा मैख़ाने से,
ला प्याला – उस में ख़ून भरूँ, ये आख़िरी जाम है।

बुरा कहो चाहे भला कहो तुम मुझे अब,
बस बताओ कहाँ शराब है – ये आख़िरी जाम है।

कसम तुम्हारी महफ़िल में फिर न आऊँगा,
अब और उनकी बातें न करो – ये आख़िरी जाम है।

कौन जाने क्या जन्नत है, क्या है दोज़ख,
तू शराब-ए-रंग-ओ-ख़ुशबू देख – ये आख़िरी जाम है।

Barsaat...

Sukhe patte ab chaahein, aur barsaat ho,
Gale milkar ek baar royen, aur barsaat ho.

Ek baar choom loon teri peshani ko main,
Sirhaane chaand aa baithe, aur raat ho.

Jaankar chalta hoon main dheere dheere,
Do pal aur mil jaayen, thodi aur baat ho.

Roz nikalta hoon wahi ittar pehenkar,
Jaane tum kahaan milo, aur mulaqaat ho.

Yun na samjho kisi ko faqeer ya shah janaab,
Kya pata kiski kya sachchai, kya haalat ho.

Tum chal lo jahaan se nange paaon,
Pata-pata khil uthe, aur roshan kaaynaat ho.

बरसात...

सूखे पत्ते अब चाहें, और बरसात हो,
गले मिलकर एक बार रोएँ, और बरसात हो।

एक बार चूम लूँ तेरी पेशानी को मैं,
सिरहाने चाँद आ बैठे, और रात हो।

जानकर चलता हूँ मैं धीरे-धीरे,
दो पल और मिल जाएँ, थोड़ी और बात हो।

रोज़ निकलता हूँ वही इत्तर पहनकर,
जाने तुम कहाँ मिलो, और मुलाक़ात हो।

यूँ न समझो किसी को फ़क़ीर या शाह जनाब,
क्या पता किसकी क्या सच्चाई, क्या हालत हो।

तुम चल लो जहाँ से नंगे पाँव,
पत्ता-पत्ता खिल उठे, और रोशन कायनात हो।

INTEZAAR इंतज़ार

Hum intezaar mein is liye nahin,

Kyunki tumne aane ka vaada kiya tha,

Hum intezaar mein hain,

Kyunki humne raah dekhne ka vaada kiya tha…

हम इंतज़ार में इसलिए नहीं,

क्योंकि तुमने आने का वादा किया था,

हम इंतज़ार में हैं,

क्योंकि हमने राह देखने का वादा किया था।

Kaun Hai?

Hum kaun hain,
Hum ek doosre se poochte hain.

Kya ye sukoon hai
Jo hota hai jab haath mein haath aate hain?

Kahin pyaar toh nahin
Jo pal bhar na dekhen toh dono ke dil tham jaate hain?

Kisi ko shaq na ho jaaye,
Toh chai bhi saare doston ke saath hi peene jaate hain.

Dard sa kuch hota hai
Jab koi unhein dekhe ya woh kisi aur ki baat par hanste hain.

Hum kaun hain,
Hum ek doosre se poochte hain.

"Chalo, kha le ab?"
Poori subah hum yahi sunne mein kaat dete hain.

Bas woh keh de "ho jaayega,"
Himmat aa jaati hai, hum duniya se jeet jaate hain.

Dost, saathi, sanam ya ajnabi —
Hum kya hain — hum khuda se poochte jaate hain.

Main likhta hoon na jaane kya,
Woh padh kar sirf ek "ji" likhen, aur dil jeet jaate hain.

Dard uthta yun — na aag, na dhuan,
Dil bhar aaye toh hum rone ko ghar se thoda door chale jaate hain.

कौन है?

हम कौन हैं,
हम एक दूसरे से पूछते हैं।

क्या ये सुकून है
जो होता है जब हाथ में हाथ आते हैं?

कहीं प्यार तो नहीं
जो पल भर न देखें तो दोनों के दिल थम जाते हैं?

किसी को शक न हो जाए,
तो चाय भी सारे दोस्तों के साथ ही पीने जाते हैं।

दर्द सा कुछ होता है
जब कोई उन्हें देखे या वो किसी और की बात पर हँसते हैं।

हम कौन हैं,
हम एक दूसरे से पूछते हैं।

"चलो, खा ले अब?"
पूरी सुबह हम यही सुनने में काट देते हैं।

बस वो कह दे "हो जाएगा,"
हिम्मत आ जाती है, हम दुनिया से जीत जाते हैं।

दोस्त, साथी, सनम या अजनबी –
हम क्या हैं – हम खुदा से पूछते जाते हैं।

मैं लिखता हूँ न जाने क्या,
वो पढ़ कर सिर्फ एक "जी" लिखें, और दिल जीत जाते हैं।

दर्द उठता यूँ – न आग, न धुआँ,
दिल भर आए तो हम रोने को घर से थोड़ा दूर चले जाते हैं।

Kahan Ho Tum?

Pooch loon chahe jahaan se ki mere jahaan ho tum,
Kahaan le gaye mujhe saath apne — ab kahaan ho tum.

Shab-o-shaam, gham-o-aab ya titliyon mein,
Kahaan hai tera noor-e-nazar, aur kyun nihaan ho tum?

Labrez hai tar-b-tar dil ab ranjish-e-aansoo se,
Tum ho saaqi, ya ho pyaala-o-jaam — kaho kaun ho tum?

Haath na aao jaise narm dhoop ho sardi ki,
Khwaab ho, khayaal ho, ya ishq ki rawaan ho tum?

Aankhon ko jhooth sikha diya aur sach ko dooba diya,
Main aapka bolta gaya — ab toh meri zubaan ho tum.

Muntazir, ab itna bhi na itrao dil tod ke apna khud,
Ishq-e-yaar khuda tumhara, farishta nahi fakt insaan ho tum.

कहाँ हो तुम?

पूछ लूँ चाहे जहाँ से कि मेरे जहाँ हो तुम,
कहाँ ले गए मुझे साथ अपने – अब कहाँ हो तुम।

शब-ओ-शाम, ग़म-ओ-आब या तितलियों में,
कहाँ है तेरा नूर-ए-नज़र, और क्यों निहाँ हो तुम?

लबरेज़ है तर-ब-तर दिल अब रंजिश-ए-आँसू से,
तुम हो साक़ी, या हो प्याला-ओ-जाम – कहो कौन हो तुम?

हाथ न आओ जैसे नरम धूप हो सर्दी की,
ख़्वाब हो, ख़याल हो, या इश्क़ की रवाँ हो तुम?

आँखों को झूठ सिखा दिया और सच को डुबो दिया,
मैं आपका बोलता गया – अब तो मेरी ज़ुबान हो तुम।

मुन्तज़िर, अब इतना भी न इतराओ दिल तोड़ के अपना ख़ुद,
इश्क़-ए-यार ख़ुदा तुम्हारा, फ़रिश्ता नहीं फ़क़्त इंसान हो तुम।

Tu Mera Kaun Hai?

Main aaina dekhta hoon,
Mujhe tu dikhta hai.

Main kaagaz dhoondta hoon,
Tu rooh par likhta hai.

Main zabaan bhool jaata hoon,
Tu aankhon se bolta hai.

Main intezaar mein jeeta hoon,
Tu bewaqt aa jaata hai.

Main kehne se jhijhakta hoon,
Tu bin bole sunta hai.

Kaise kahun tujhse ki tu mera kya lagta hai.

Main gale lagana chahta hoon,
Tu sirf khwaab mein milta hai.

God mein sir rakh chain se sota hoon,
Tu saare gham pee jaata hai.

Mere bas ki nahi ki ab kaabu karoon,
Tu khushboo sa jo phailta hai.

Koi toh bataye ab aur kya kahun main,
Jab tu hi nahi jaanta ki tu mera kaun hai.

तू मेरा कौन है?

पूछ लूँ चाहे जहाँ से कि मेरे जहाँ हो तुम,
कहाँ ले गए मुझे साथ अपने – अब कहाँ हो तुम।

शब-ओ-शाम, ग़म-ओ-आब या तितलियों में,
कहाँ है तेरा नूर-ए-नज़र, और क्यों निहाँ हो तुम?

लबरेज़ है तर-ब-तर दिल अब रंजिश-ए-आँसू से,
तुम हो साक़ी, या हो प्याला-ओ-जाम – कहो कौन हो तुम?

हाथ न आओ जैसे नरम धूप हो सर्दी की,
ख़्वाब हो, ख़याल हो, या इश्क़ की रवाँ हो तुम?

आँखों को झूठ सिखा दिया और सच को डुबो दिया,
मैं आपका बोलता गया – अब तो मेरी ज़ुबान हो तुम।

मुन्तज़िर, अब इतना भी न इतराओ दिल तोड़ के अपना ख़ुद,
इश्क़-ए-यार ख़ुदा तुम्हारा, फ़रिश्ता नहीं फ़क़्त इंसान हो तुम।

PAL

Ek pal ke sau hisse kar do,
Har hisse mein sau baar yaad aati hai.

Phir sochta hoon ek baar ko bhool jaoon,
Ek baar bhoolne pe sau baar yaad aati hai.

Tu gair hai mujhse — iska gham nahi,
Gair hoke bhi kyun apnon sa yaad aati hai?

Din bhar toh chai aur kaam se kaam chala leta hoon,
Shaam hote hote mujhe phir sharaab yaad aati hai.

Aansu rok loon kaise aur kya dil patthar karoon,
Dard se hans deta hoon jab jab teri yaad aati hai.

पल

एक पल के सौ हिस्से कर दो,
हर हिस्से में सौ बार याद आती है।

फिर सोचता हूँ एक बार को भूल जाऊँ,
एक बार भूलने पे सौ बार याद आती है।

तू ग़ैर है मुझसे – इसका ग़म नहीं,
ग़ैर होकर भी क्यों अपनों सा याद आती है?

दिन भर तो चाय और काम से काम चला लेता हूँ,
शाम होते होते मुझे फिर शराब याद आती है।

आँसू रोक लूँ कैसे और क्या दिल पत्थर करूँ,
दर्द से हँस देता हूँ जब जब तेरी याद आती है।

Yaad Nahi...

Ji kuch dhoondh raha hoon main, mujhe yaad nahi,
Aakhri baar kahan dekha tha, mujhe yaad nahi.

Woh baarish ki shaam jab tum milne aaye the,
Kyun dil do pal ko behka tha, mujhe yaad nahi.

Hai ek toota sa ghar us dasht-e-sheher mein,
Teri yaad ke siwa kaun rehta tha, mujhe yaad nahi.

Dard itna ke rooh kaanpe, par uff na kiya,
Kyun bin matlab dard sehta tha, mujhe yaad nahi.

Tum chahti ho mujhe kamyaab-o-khush-o-muqammal dekhna,
Kis dar pe rakh aaya hoon mera fann-o-hunur-o-hosla, mujhe yaad nahi.

Muntazir roz dhoondhta hoon unki aankhon mein pyaar,
Pichhli baar kab unki aankhon mein dekha, mujhe yaad nahi.

याद नहीं

जी कुछ ढूँढ़ रहा हूँ मैं, मुझे याद नहीं,
आख़िरी बार कहाँ देखा था, मुझे याद नहीं।

वो बारिश की शाम जब तुम मिलने आए थे,
क्यों दिल दो पल को बहका था, मुझे याद नहीं।

है एक टूटा सा घर उस दश्त-ए-शहर में,
तेरी याद के सिवा कौन रहता था, मुझे याद नहीं।

दर्द इतना कि रूह काँपे, पर उफ़ न किया,
क्यों बिन मतलब दर्द सहता था, मुझे याद नहीं।

तुम चाहती हो मुझे कामयाब-ओ-खुश-ओ-मुकम्मल देखना,
किस दर पे रख आया हूँ मेरा फ़न-ओ-हुनर-ओ-हौसला, मुझे याद नहीं।

मुन्तज़िर रोज़ ढूँढ़ता हूँ उनकी आँखों में प्यार,
पिछली बार कब उनकी आँखों में देखा, मुझे याद नहीं।

Yun Na Thi...

Yun na thi kismat ki baahon mein yaar hota,
Gul hote gulshan mein, sada-bahaar kaisa hota?

Kuch toh khuda bhi zyada nahin chahta humein,
Aur kya wajah hoti ke humein phir se pyaar hota?

Tu bulaati mujhe, main kaanton pe chal kar aata,
Teri aankhon ka nasha phir dil par sawaar hota.

Fareb aur sansani hi bikte hain aaj kal,
Deen-o-imaan se likhte, toh kya aisa akhbaar hota?

Tum hote toh kya gham-e-zindagi hota,
Pyaar bikta, aur khushi ka karobaar hota.

Kya kahun — jalta hoon auron ko dekh dekh,
Kaash mera bhi koi aashiq, koi jaan-nisaar hota.

यूँ न थी

यूँ न थी किस्मत की बाँहों में यार होता,
गुल होते गुलशन में, सदा-बहार कैसा होता?

कुछ तो ख़ुदा भी ज़्यादा नहीं चाहता हमें,
और क्या वजह होती कि हमें फिर से प्यार होता?

तू बुलाती मुझे, मैं काँटों पे चल कर आता,
तेरी आँखों का नशा फिर दिल पर सवार होता।

फ़रेब और सनसनी ही बिकते हैं आजकल,
दीन-ओ-ईमान से लिखते, तो क्या ऐसा अख़बार होता?

तुम होते तो क्या ग़म-ए-ज़िंदगी होता,
प्यार बिकता, और खुशी का कारोबार होता।

क्या कहूँ – जलता हूँ औरों को देख देख,
काश मेरा भी कोई आशिक़, कोई जान-निसार होता।

शुक्रिया...

अगर इन पन्नों में कहीं
आपको अपना दिल धड़कता सुनाई दिया हो,
तो यूँ ही ख़ामोश मत हो जाइए।

जुड़े रहिए...
कभी एक ख़त बनकर,
कभी एक पैग़ाम बनकर।

मैं यहीं रहूँगा –
उसी जगह,
उसी इंतज़ार में।

क्योंकि नाम ही मेरा
मुन्तज़िर है।

आप मुझ तक पहुँच सकते हैं:

ईमेल: write2muntazir@gmail.com
इंस्टाग्राम: @the.reluctant.superhero

About the Author

Deepak Parmar is an entrepreneur, education innovator, and writer whose work sits at the intersection of ideas, learning, and human stories. Over the past two decades, he has built and led initiatives in higher education, career services, and skills development, working closely with universities, institutions, and industry to improve pathways between education and employment. He is the cofounder of Aimerz.ai and has been involved in designing large-scale programs focused on student outcomes, career readiness, and new models of applied learning.

Alongside his work in education, Parmar has long maintained a quiet relationship with poetry. Influenced by the emotional depth of Urdu poetry and the reflective minimalism of modern verse, his writing explores themes of longing, love, separation, and the fragile inner conversations people carry with themselves. His poems often inhabit the spaces between words: pauses, memories, and moments that remain unresolved yet deeply felt.

Muntazir is his debut poetry collection. The book brings together poems written over several years and is structured around four emotional movements—*Intezaar* (Waiting), *Guftagu* (Conversations), *Firaaq* (Separation), and Sukoon (Stillness). Through these sections, Parmar traces the emotional arc of love and absence, capturing the quiet persistence of memory and the strange tenderness of waiting.

He currently lives and works in India, where he continues to build education ventures while writing poetry in the spaces between work, travel, and thought.

www.ingramcontent.com/pod-product-compliance
Lightning Source LLC
LaVergne TN
LVHW100326210926
848480LV00003B/1275